Modern
Glass

Modern
Glass

Ronald
Stennett-Willson

Studio Vista

The author wishes to thank Wedgwood Glass for kindly supplying many of the
photographs shown in this book.

Title page illustration
Pressed glass plate used as hanging window
decoration. Designed by Tamara Aladin and made by
Riihimaen Lasi Oy, Finland

Studio Vista
An imprint of Cassell & Collier Macmillan Publishers Ltd.,
35 Red Lion Square, London WC1R 4SG,
and at Sydney, Auckland, Toronto, Johannesburg,
an affiliate of Macmillan Inc., New York

ISBN 0 289 70573 8

Designed by Ian Craig
Set in 12pt Univers 685 1pt leaded
Printed by Colour Reproductions Ltd., Billericay, Essex
Bound by Webb Son & Co. Ltd.

Contents

Long tailed birds in
various colours.
Designed by Ronald
Stennett-Willson and
made by Wedgwood
Glass, England

Mushroom paperweights made free-hand in brown and white with speckled tops. Designed by Ronald Stennett-Willson and made by Wedgwood Glass, England

Introduction

Although the glass maker's craft goes back 3,500−4,000 years, there does not appear to be any evidence that glass was blown before the Phoenicians of 2,000 years ago. In essence the craft cannot have changed much since that time. The hand-made glass industry is one where the old methods of craftsmanship cannot be replaced by new mechanical ones.

Glass in its natural form was used by man many thousands of years before he discovered how to make it himself. For instance, in the form of minerals such as Obsidian, a shiny black rock of volcanic origin, this was used by our Stone Age ancestors to make arrow heads, knives and axes. Another natural glass is Fulgurite, which is created by lightning striking loose sands or rocks.

It is unlikely that we shall ever know where man-made glass originated, but we do have an account by the Roman historian Pliny, writing in the first century A.D., of an accidental discovery of glass by a party of merchants who were carrying a cargo of Natron, that is, crude soda. When, on the beach at the mouth of the river Belus in Phoenicia, they were cooking a meal and could not find any stones with which to prop up their cooking pots, they used lumps of soda from their cargo. When these lumps melted and mingled with the sand 'transparent streams of a strange liquid were seen to flow'—and thus glass was discovered! This story does seem more myth than factual historical account. One cannot help feeling that if they had generated enough heat to

melt sand their meal would have been rather overcooked. However, there is a possible element of truth in Pliny's account because glass was and still is, basically made from silica (sand, flints or crushed quartz), alkili (natural soda or plant ash) and a stabilizer such as limestone. It is also known that sand from the river Belus was famous, in ancient times, for glass making.

The earliest records of glass technology come from Mesopotamia and these are in the form of cuneiform inscriptions on clay tablets. The first of these date back to the seventeenth century B.C. but suggest that glass making was already well established. In 4,000 B.C., in Egypt and Mesopotamia, vitreous glazes were used for covering pottery or stone, mostly in order to create the effect of precious or semi-precious stones.

Egypt can certainly claim the earliest known glass furnace, which was found by Sir Flinders Petrie in 1891 at Tell el Amarna. This was the remains of a glass works ascribed to about 1,350 B.C., but the earliest hollow glass vessels found are dated to the Egypt of around 1,500 B.C. These first hollow pieces were apparently made by using the sand core method. A core of sand or clay was attached to the end of a metal rod and then coated with glass, either by dipping it into a crucible of molten glass or by winding glass threads around it. The piece was then made smooth by continuous reheating or 'marvering', that is, by rolling the object on a flat smooth surface. It would appear that it was during the first century B.C. that the blowing iron was first used. It was this major step forward, which gave a man the ability to manipulate a blown glass bubble, that gave to glass making the possibility of being the diverse and fascinating craft that it still is. Yet, although that basic part of the glass maker's art remains unchanged, modern technology has given him possibilities previously unthought of. Because the material itself has been improved, the glass maker's craft has been enlarged and more opportunity given to him to develop individual ingenuity and skill.

The craft of the glass maker must be almost unique in that modern technology has enabled glassware to be made which is quite different from that made for centuries, yet still using the same tools and methods. It is true that automatic and semi-automatic machines can make drinking glasses, bowls and vases in large, even vast quantities, and when this glassware is well designed for its purpose, it is very satisfactory. But such glassware, by the nature of its production, is limited and a small glass factory making glass by hand with skilled workers has a flexibility which allows it to turn out an astonishing variety of articles in surprisingly large quantities.

In times past the glass factories were sited in the forests which provided the fuel for the furnaces, the glass makers being itinerant, burning the trees around them and then moving on. This practice was forbidden in England in the beginning of the seventeenth century and coal was developed as a fuel. Wood was still being used as a fuel in countries such as Sweden up to the beginning of this century. In many countries, Great Britain and Belgium for example, the forest has long gone from around the factories, but although a present-day factory may melt its glass by oil, gas or electricity, the pattern of work inside the glass house is very much the same

as it has always been. A busy glass house with its workers clustered around the furnace which contains pots of molten glass, the constant movement of the inner circle of men working at the furnace openings, gathering glass from the pots, blowing and working the glowing semi-liquid, and the slower rhythm of those working on the perimeter of the circle 'bearing in' (that is, taking the hot articles away), the heat and light from the fiery furnace openings and glory holes, the clatter of solidified glass being hammered from the ends of used blowing irons and the tracks of light which trace the passage of men carrying a blob of molten glass on an iron pipe, combine into a spectacle of sight, sound and rhythm which never palls.

Although there are variations from country to country, most glass works are made to a similar pattern. This pattern has changed, but only a little, during the last few years. Traditionally the heart of the glass house was one or more large beehive-shaped furnaces, heated from beneath and holding six, eight or ten pots of glass. There is now a tendency for factories to use single pot furnaces, which means that there can be more control in the firing of individual pots of glass.

The pot in which the glass is melted is, in itself, a remarkable piece of work. It is made by hand over many weeks, of a particular mixture of fireclays, and is allowed to dry out most carefully under controlled temperature. It can itself weigh up to a ton and will hold half a ton of molten glass, frequently more. The men who make the glass pots are specialists and in times past they were itinerant, travelling from factory to factory and making many months supply of pots before moving on. When the factory needs to use a new pot it is placed in a large kiln called an 'arch'. This fires the pot on a carefully calculated, controlled upward curve of temperature to between 1400°C. and 1500°C. When the pot is ready the front of the glass furnace is broken down, the old pot removed, and the new pot put speedily in as near to its highest temperature as possible. This is a sight rarely seen by people who do not work in a glass factory. It is always impressive and, when sometimes things do not go quite smoothly, even dramatic.

With the increasing use of single pot furnaces more factories are melting glass overnight, although there are still many which melt over a period of forty-eight hours. The time depends to a great extent on the kind of glass being melted. In a modern factory which melts overnight, the pots will be 'charged' with the 'batch' at the end of the working day, when the glass makers have left and the furnace men take over. This means that the pots—which have probably been 'worked out' or emptied during the day—are filled with a mixture of sand, soda, lime, with other ingredients and additions according to the kind of glass required (such as lead oxide if the factory is making a brilliant lead crystal). Most famous factories have their own jealously guarded recipes which produce a glass, or 'metal', which is characteristic of their own production and is frequently recognizable. This also applies when colours are melted. The glass technologist has had to devise new recipes to replace the traditional ones for the various coloured glasses, as some of the chemicals, rare earths, or metal oxides have become scarce or too expensive. (There was a time for instance, when a gold ruby glass was obtained by the addition of gold to the molten glass in the pot.) It may be said that glass colours are not what they used to be, but there is a far greater variety of transparent and opaque colours available to glass makers than previously was the case. This mixture is shovelled in through the

mouth of the pot and the furnace temperature is pushed up as rapidly as possible to 1400°C. or more, until the added batch has melted and turned to glass. The furnaces are watched and the temperature controlled all through the night. One or two hours before the glass makers are due to start work, usually very early in the day, the glass is cooled down to the working temperature, about 1000°-1100°C., according to the glass makers' requirements, and allowed to settle. Glass melting can now be controlled by electronic instruments, which means that the quality of the molten glass can be kept consistent. Previously, the temperature deep inside the pot of melting glass had to be estimated by eye, the judgment of the furnace man, or at best by instruments which were only approximately accurate. The hand adjustments to the fuel supply were largely governed by trial and error, and there was an inevitable time lag between the adjustment being made and the temperature changing in the furnace. New instruments can control the supply of fuel and air in precise quantities, to maintain a flame of the heat required at any particular moment of the melting cycle. This means that a good supply of clear glass, free from 'seeds' (minute bubbles) or 'cords' (glass of varying consistency which shows striations in the finished piece), is a daily certainty instead of a hoped for possibility. This specialized work of glass melting requires considerable technical knowledge and care, and is very important to the factory, for every glass maker comes to work each morning expecting to have a pot of good glass to work on.

Usually one man of top skill is served by four or five, or even six or seven others, according to the custom of the factory or country. This group of workers is called a 'chair' or 'shop', the senior or most skilled being the master or gaffer. The others serve the gaffer by gathering from the furnace, partially working the glass or, in the making of wine glasses, some will blow the bowl while others gather glass for the stem and foot. The gaffer usually makes the stem and foot, although sometimes he just makes the stem and another member of the chair makes the foot.

Gathering the glass, which is the first act of the glass maker, is one requiring a considerable skill and one which is not always obvious. One cannot linger long at the furnace opening because of the radiated heat, and someone else is invariably waiting to come and gather. The blowing iron, which is a steel tube, four to five feet long, usually longer in Britain, has a wedge-shaped nose on one end and these vary in size according to the kind of articles being made. The gather must be made from the surface of the glass in the centre of the pot and must cause the minimum disturbance. Clumsy gathering can spoil the glass for other workers. With a deft twist of the iron the blower dips it into the glass and revolves it between his fingers, collecting a blob of molten glass on the end. He then goes with this to the 'marver', which was a slab of marble in times past and in some small factories still is. Now it is more usually a very highly polished slab of hard steel. On this the blower rolls the glass into a wedge-shaped cylinder. Then comes a most exciting moment and one which is usually missed by a spectator in a glass works: the blower blows down the iron and quickly puts his thumb over the mouth piece, and waits. The heat of the iron and the glass causes the air to expand and into this solid lump of glass is forced a small bubble. Until the bubble appears the glass is lifeless, but once there it can be blown larger and worked upon. This is the beginning of practically every piece of hand-made glass. From this point on there are many ways in which the glass maker can manipulate the glass bubble; mostly he will use a mould made of wood, steel or carbon, and this mould

may give the partial or complete shape of the finished article. If he is making a wine glass the mould will be the shape of the bowl of the glass and he will lower the pendant bubble into the mould, gently blowing down the iron while rapidly rotating it. The bubble of glass grows and finally overflows the top of the mould. When the glass has sufficiently cooled to hold its form it is withdrawn. If the blown shape is such that it cannot be withdrawn from the top of the mould, he signals to the apprentice who is holding the mould and the mould is opened by being split in half.

The blower now has on the end of the iron a bubble which has taken the shape of the wine glass bowl and is ready for a stem to be added. The glass may be soft enough where it joins the iron to become distorted, so the iron is never allowed to stay still but is constantly rotated, working against the force of gravity. Now another member of the team, called the 'bit gatherer', will take from the furnace on a solid steel rod, enough glass for a stem, and this is brought to the gaffer who now has the iron with the bowl attached. The gaffer guides the assistant's bit iron by holding it with the end of his shears and attaches the new glass to the bottom of the bowl. The bowl of the glass has to be cool enough not to lose its shape but not cold: the added piece of glass must not be so hot that it is too liquid to control or so cool that it cannot be worked; and so there is a limited range of temperature at which the two pieces can be brought together. Outside this range tensions may be caused which are too strong to be evened out during the annealing process. Quickly the bit iron is pulled a short distance away and the glass stretches. With the same shears the gaffer cuts off exactly the amount of glass he needs for the stem. He lays the blowing iron across the arms of his chair and rolls it back and forth, at the same time forming the stem by

10

stretching and manipulating the molten glass with a tool rather like an oversize pair of sugar-tongs. After the blowing iron this is the most used tool and is in fact called the 'tool'. The same procedure follows for the foot of the glass and when this is finished he dribbles a little cold water on to the glass where it joins the iron, gives the iron a smart tap, and the glass drops off. It is interesting to note that at this point the glass is unbelievably strong and to break it it is necessary to fracture the surface by applying cold water or metal. It does not stay like this for long and if it were allowed to cool naturally the glass would break up after a few minutes. While it is being worked it may have been cooled and re-heated many times. Pieces of hot glass may have been added to cool glass as, for instance, the handle of a jug or the stem and foot of a wine glass. This causes stresses to be set up and the thicker the glass the more this is likely. At this stage the glass is still very hot and it is carried by another member of the chair called the 'taker in' in a forked piece of wood or metal wrapped around with asbestos string to the annealing lehr. This is a long kiln through which the glass travels on a very slowly moving belt. In this it is heated up to a temperature below that at which it will melt and lose its shape, but high enough to release or even out the stresses. It is then cooled very slowly on a controlled descending temperature curve. The glass thus becomes more stable and less sensitive to sudden temperature changes. Once out of the lehr, all the rest of the work is on the exterior of the glass.

By the time the gaffer knocks off the finished glass and it is taken away, the blower has another bowl blown on an iron and this is laid on the gaffer's chair and the process is repeated. A skilled team of glass makers working very closely together can produce a wine glass in three to six minutes, although in some cases it may take longer depending on the thickness of the glass and the simplicity or otherwise of the stem.

If the article to be made is a bowl or vase the procedure can be different; a mould may possibly be used to give a partial shape or it can be made completely free-hand. It will almost certainly be necessary to use more glass than it is possible to gather initially and when the first bubble has been blown up to a size which increases its surface area and it has cooled a little, it will be taken back to the furnace and another gather made. Dextrously twisting and turning the iron to keep the glass central, sometimes using the force of gravity to help by letting the glass flow for a moment to get the shape wanted, the maker waits until the glass cools from white hot to cherry red. Gradually the glass bubble is brought to the size required and coaxed into the desired shape by the simple tools of the glass maker who manipulates the hot semi-liquid glass with a piece of wood, the tool, or frequently with his own hands protected by a pad of wet newspaper. At some stage in this way of making it may be necessary to take the piece of glass off the iron so that it can be worked on differently. To achieve this a member of the team takes a 'pontil' rod, a solid iron rod about the same length and thickness as a blowing iron, usually referred to as a 'punty', and gathers a small amount of glass on the end. This is shaped and the surplus cut away until the end of the rod is just covered with molten glass in a neat round tip. This is then pressed on the bottom of the ball of glass on the blowing iron. All this time the iron and now the pontil rod are being constantly rotated to keep the glass central. As before, the maker dribbles a little water on to a point just where the glass swells out from the blowing iron, gives the iron a rap, and the glass breaks away. It is now a bubble with a hole in

11

the top and is attached only to the pontil rod. By this time the glass has become too cold to work and it is taken to the 'glory hole', which used to be an opening in the furnace near the pot mouth but is now a separate portable piece of equipment like an open oven with a flame hot enough to melt the glass. In the heat of the glory hole the glass becomes soft enough to work again. Taking the glass back to his chair, the master glass maker will, with his shears, cut away unwanted glass from the edge and shape the piece of glass to the designer's wishes. It may be opened to form a flat dish, or it may be a jug with a shaped top and lip to which a handle will be attached. It is frequently here that the master glass maker can demonstrate his skill as it is the ability to manipulate glass at this stage that determines the degree of skill of the glass maker and his standing in the glass works.

In most glass works a chair of workers is paid according to the amount of good pieces of glass they make in a shift or stint. The money is, in effect, shared out between them relative to their skill, the more senior, skilled members receiving a higher percentage. It is therefore to the advantage of all of them to work as skilfully and as quickly as possible. The craftsmanship of a chair is shown not only in what they make but in their economy of effort and the anticipation of each member of the team's next move.

A chair is also the name given to the seat on which the glass maker sits and works. This is a bench three or four feet wide, which has arms standing out in front for about three feet. These arms turn up sharply at the end to form hooks which act as stops when the glass maker lays his iron across the arms, which he does when he sits at the chair rolling the iron backwards and forwards and working the glass with his right hand. On the right hand side of the chair, at the same height as the seat, is

a shelf on which he places the tools he is using at the time. These tools do not appear to have changed for hundreds of years and are so simple as to seem primitive. There are shears, really scissors, for cutting or 'driving' the edge of a piece of molten glass, two pairs of calipers for measuring and the 'tool', which can be in different forms, for instance with sharp edged legs for cutting down the glass before taking it off the iron, with wooden legs for shaping large pieces of glass or, though only occasionally these days, with legs of compressed paper which when wet burn down evenly without marking the glass. These tools are used much as fingers might be; the tool, and indeed all the glass maker's implements, are extensions of his own hands, of necessity, since the material he is working is a red-hot semi-fluid substance. A piece of wood, cup-shaped or flat, is used as a hand might be to shape the glass and even the hand itself is used, protected by a pad of wet newspaper.

One of the properties of molten glass is that if a pattern is imprinted on it when it is soft, however much the glass is twisted and stretched, some trace of the pattern remains. This characteristic is frequently used in the making of decorative glass or the fancy stems of wine glasses. Some of the devices which a glass maker can use to exploit this quality are extremely simple. For instance, a piece of wood with nails driven into it, on which the glass is pressed at a certain stage, will leave an impression on the glass which can survive all the manipulations or re-heating the glass may go through, and finally appear as decoration on the finished article.

A further property is that glass can enclose air and that the additional internal surface areas reflect light. The random insertion of air can be achieved in many ways and is relatively easy, for instance, directing a jet of cold air on to a solid lump of hot glass will cause air bubbles to form inside. The pattern they take, will of course, be unpredictable; to insert air in a precise form and place in the glass needs considerable skill and a few experienced glass makers have their own methods.

A combined candlestick and flower bowl with an interesting treatment to the foot. Designed by Nanny Still and made by Riihimaen Lasi Oy, Finland

Design

Glass is a material that has had in the past very definite limitations for those who work it. Museums are full of pieces of glass which, while illustrating the skill of designers or workers, also demonstrate how this skill has been severely limited by the quality of glass. The glass worker of today has a considerable advantage over his predecessors in that there has been a great increase of technical knowledge and this has given him a choice of several different kinds of glass. He has glasses which are melted to suit different purposes, some which are soft and brilliant and can be surface cut more easily, some which are harder and can be blown more thinly, some which can be toughened to withstand heat and can be used for cooking vessels. These different kinds of glass are classified very roughly as lead crystal, soda lime and borosilicate glasses.

Most students of glass know of the work of Ravenscroft in England in the second half of the seventeenth century, when he set to work to try to find the formula for a glass which would have brilliance, transparency and strength and which would remain stable. He finally succeeded in compounding a mixture of materials which had lead oxide added to it. This resulted, eventually, in a glass which was much better than anything melted previously and was the beginning of what we know as lead crystal. During the past sixty years, the quality of glass has improved beyond anything known before, particularly in the purity which it is possible to attain. It is the appearance of a piece of lead crystal, with a pure clear surface holding the light, which has prompted many designers to exploit all the possible qualities of the material.

The most valued gift that science has given to the glass maker is control. As we have seen it is possible for him now to know very accurately what will come out of the pot of glass in the furnace because the materials which go into it are measured and graded more accurately. The furnace temperature can be controlled more precisely (even from minute to minute) during the melting process. The lehr or kiln in which the glass is annealed or cooled is also controlled with precision. Firing with oil, gas or electricity and the use of sophisticated electronic controlling instruments have made this possible.

The improved quality of the basic raw material has given increased opportunities to designers, and in turn to keep pace with the demands of designers glass makers have been forced more fully to exploit the craft which lies in their hands. It is remarkable how much skill glass makers have developed in response to this demand.

The designer of glass stands in a different relationship to the material with which he works from almost all other designers. He is usually at one remove. He must work with an intimate knowledge of the process of making, but he need not himself be able to blow glass or work it. It is rarely given to one man to be able to blow glass

15

or work it free-hand, cut, engrave and design. Indeed if he had the ability, it is unlikely that he would have the opportunity. The glass blower actually makes the glass and the craftsman-designer is usually the one who designs. There are two results of this; firstly, the artist seeking the satisfaction that comes from working out his own designs with his own hands rarely turns to glass; and secondly, the highest artistic quality of glass coming from the average glass factory is usually at the level of the artistic ability of their most skilled worker (that is, assuming he is allowed licence to make what he wishes). It is only where a designer or someone with discrimination is given authority that this is otherwise. For a factory to produce well-designed glass, someone has to be brought in who has the ability to see the possibilities of the material, who can grasp the significance of the processes and who can achieve the kind of relationship with the craftsmen that will enable him, through their hands, to translate his ideas into form. For a glass designer to be successful he must be able to work alongside a glass maker and stay there for long periods, for it is only in this way that the possibilities are to be seen. Between the moment when the gather of molten glass is first made on the blowing iron and the moment when an article is finally formed, there are innumerable possibilities which cannot be conceived unless the artist is continually on the spot. It is those factories which have given a measure of authority to the practical mind of the artist-designer that produce today's really good modern glass. This is particularly true of the Scandanavian countries and of Sweden above all.

However, a most welcome development during the last ten years has been the increase in the number of individual designer-craftsmen working in glass. This has been the result of colleges in Britain and America starting Glass Departments. This has given those with the talent to do so, the opportunity to design and make their own glass. Just from a technical point of view, the glass which a man working alone can produce is very limited and it is to be hoped that those who start alone, and make, with difficulty, interesting pieces, will take their work a stage further by combining with others who have a similar skill. We may then see the growth of 'Glass Workshops' in which three or four craftsmen work together; workshops large enough to be economically successful and small enough to be able to concentrate on making individual pieces of glass to the highest possible standards of craftsmanship and design. Such pieces would be on a par with fine quality painting or sculpture.

When one looks at many pieces of modern glass, it is evident that many designers have become excited by the possible beauty of the glass itself and, instead of making it into a drinking vessel or a vase to be decorated by cutting in the traditional manner, they have begun to make shapes which exploit the aesthetic properties of the medium, its transparency, the fact that it can carry colours either transparent or opaque, its ability to reflect light, its smoothness and crystalline nature, and contradictory appearance of solidified liquidity. In many forms it can have a startling quality of arrested movement.

Once a master glass maker has on the end of a blowing iron a dully glowing bubble of glass gently expanding under the pressure of his breath, twisting and turning as he keeps it moving to resist or to use the force of gravity, there are an incalculable number of shapes which the bubble can take: many pieces of the present day reflect the glass designer's awareness of this, and in many of them there is evidence of that miraculous moment when the liquid glass changes to a solid. Other designers have sought to decorate glass in such a manner that its natural properties are added to and enhanced. To the arts of the cutter and engraver have been added sand blasting and acid etching. Decorating by enamels fired to the glass is not a new process but it has only recently become possible to silkscreen directly on to the glass and this has enabled the glass decorator to use his ingenuity to produce well designed decorated glass more cheaply.

Many factories have their own precious processes which they have invented or devised both for decorating and making glass, and these will no doubt be increased as more and more is discovered about this fascinating material.

Today, glass offers a possibility and a tremendous challenge to those designers, glass makers and manufacturers who wish to express their ideas and craftsmanship in this, one of the oldest and yet, one of the newest of media.

A copper wheel engraved bowl entitled 'State Flower Bowl'. Designed by Asta Strömberg and made by Strömbergshyttan, Sweden

Designers and manufacturers

Tamara Aladin	Finland
Olle Alberius	Sweden
Sergio Asti	Italy
Masakichi Awashima	Japan
Lisa Bauer	Sweden
G. Baxter MSIAD	England
W. Bernstein	America
Severin Brøby	Norway
John Cook	England
John Coughlan	England
Robert Couterier	France
Donald Crowley	America
Salvador Dali	France
Patricia Davidson	America
Jean-Pierre Demardi	France
Peter Dreiser	England
Elly Eliades	England
Kay Franck	Finland
Jane Gilchrist	England
Michael Harris	England
Lars Hellston	Sweden
Paul Hlava	Czechoslovakia
Günther Hofmann	Germany
Erik Höglund	Sweden
Christel & Christer Holmgren	Denmark
James Houston	America
John Hutton	England
Edward Iglehart	Scotland
Jan Johansson	Sweden
Birgitta Karlsson	Italy
Professor Klingg	Czechoslovakia
Dominick Labino	America
Marie Claude Lalique	France
Marc Lalique	France
Vicke Lindstrand	Sweden
Marvin Lipovsky	America
Vera Liskova	Czechoslovakia
Per Lütken	Denmark
Josephine Majella	England
Annette Meech	England
Kimrie Newcomb	America
Sven Palmqvist	Sweden
Sigurd Persson	Sweden
Don Pollard	America

ulpture in clear crystal
h eye in red and blue.
signed by Göran
arff and made by
sta-Boda
assworks, Sweden

Robert Rigot	France
Paul Schulze	America
Alexander Seidel	America
David Smith	England
Ronald Stennett-Willson	England
Nanny Still	Finland
Rune Strand	Sweden
Asta Strömberg	Sweden
Josef Svarc	Czechoslovakia
Colin Terris	Scotland
George Thompson	America
Ove Thorsen	Italy
Frank Thrower	England
Oiva Toikka	Finland
Bertil Vallén	Sweden
Bruce Walker	Scotland
Ann Wärff	Sweden
Göran Wärff	Sweden
Sidse Werner	Denmark
Uno Westerberg	Sweden
Laurence Whistler	England
Toni Zuccheri	Italy

Arabia Glassworks	Finland
Awashima Glass	Japan
Baccarat	France
Bohemia Glassworks	Czechoslovakia
Caithness Glass	Scotland
Ceskycristal Vcelnicka Glassworks	Czechoslovakia
Dartington Glass	England
Daum	France
Hadelands Glassworks	Norway
Holmegaard Glassworks	Denmark
T & W Ide	England
Isle of Wight Studio Glass	England
Kosta–Boda	Sweden
Cristal Lalique	France
Glasshütte Leichlingen	Germany
Moser Glassworks	Czechoslovakia
Nötsjö Glass	Finland
Orrefors Glassworks	Sweden
Peill & Pützler	Germany
Pukebergs Glassworks	Sweden
Riihimaen Lasi	Finland
Schott-Zwiesel	Germany
Steuben Glass	America
Strömbergshyttan	Sweden
Uzilkovlesklo N.C.	Czechoslovakia
Venini	Italy
Webb Corbett	England
Wedgwood Glass	England
Whitefriars Glass	England

Making a wine glass

Making a wine glass by hand requires the use of many aspects of the glass maker's skill.

Judgment is required to gather just the right amount of glass from the furnace. The ball of glass needs to be formed carefully before blowing; and the blowing of the glass into the mould must be accomplished in such a way that it leaves it cleanly, at a temperature that is low enough for it not to distort and yet not too cool for the rest of the work to be done. The adding of glass to glass in the manipulation or tooling of extra pieces to form the stem and foot also demands great expertise.

After the glass maker has finished his work there come the finishing processes. There are three stages in the finishing of a wine glass once it has passed the quality control. Firstly, the top of the glass where it was attached to the blowing iron is 'cracked off'. It is scored with a diamond or tungsten point, revolves on a small turntable with a fine glass flame playing on the incised line, and after a few seconds the top cracks off remarkably evenly. Secondly, the now sharp edge has to be made smooth and this is done by applying the edge to a moving band of fine carborundum under a spray of water. The edge of the glass is now smooth but matt and the third stage in the finishing process is to melt this edge. The glass is placed on a revolving disc, on a revolving platform which carries it through a series of gas flames in order to melt the edge sufficiently to give a soft polished surface.

There are machines which will carry out all these processes automatically and quickly but where a factory is making a diverse range of articles which will have different heights and thickness there is no substitute for the individual attention and judgment given to each stage by a skilled worker.

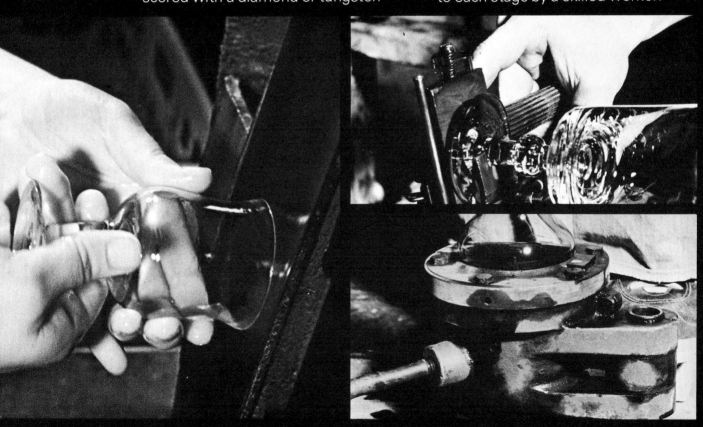

The blower goes to the furnace for the initial gather of glass

This is 'marvered' into shape

The air is blown into the solid lump of glass, the blower's thumb sealing the end of the blowing iron

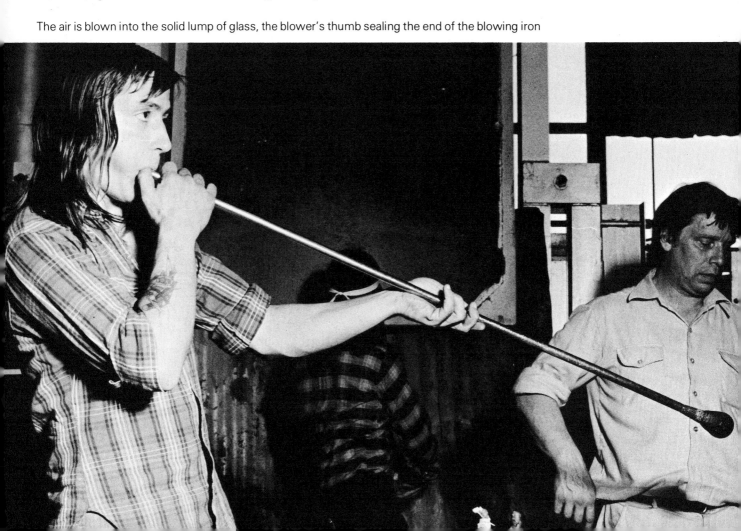

The enlarged bubble is lowered into the mould
which will give the shape of the wine glass bowl

A gather of glass is added to the bowl from which
the gaffer will form the stem

The glass has been blown to fill the mould

The stem is being tooled into shape

A further gather is being cut away from the 'bit iron' to form the foot

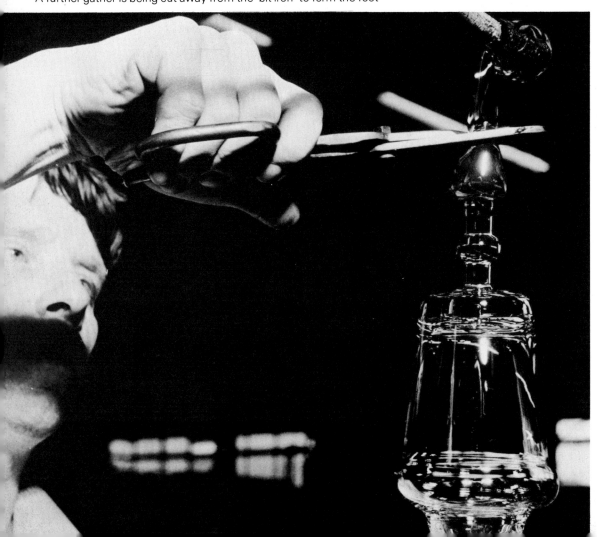

The foot is made using a modern adjustable foot tool

The foot is finally made true with a piece of wood before being broken off the iron, and taken to the lehr for annealing

Opposite top
After passing through the lehr each glass is inspected for quality of material and quality of making before going through the final finishing processes

Opposite bottom
After 'cracking off' (see preamble above), the sharp edge is made smooth by the application of a moving band of fine carborundum

Below
In the third stage after quality control, the matt edge is melted by a series of gas flames to give a soft polished surface

Many Scandinavian factories make these small sized decanters, used for schnapps. This one is stoppered with a cork and metal ring of traditional style. Designed by Nanny Still and made by Riimimaen Lasi Oy, Finland

Table glass

Many pieces of glass appear on the table—wine glasses, bowls for flowers or fruit, candlesticks for the dinner table—but the term table glass is generally accepted to mean the decanters, jugs and drinking glasses which go to make up a table suite or wine service.

Most experienced glass designers will agree that a wine service is very difficult to design. Each glass has to have a relationship with the other pieces. It is not enough to make a glass with the same shape merely larger or smaller. The proportions may have to be altered quite subtly to make it appear that the same glass has been made in different sizes.

Very few factories now make wine services with a range of glasses designed to cope with every kind of drink. Table glass today is rather more suited to our smaller dining tables and our more flexible way of eating or entertaining. A wine service will now consist of four or five glasses, a goblet for water or beer, a wine glass for red or white wine, a glass for champagne, a glass which can be used for sherry or port or even cocktails and possibly a fifth glass for a liqueur. Of course a lot depends on the country, because there are national preferences to be taken into account.

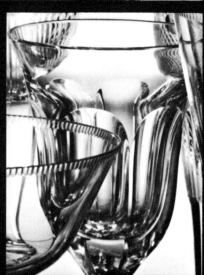

Stoppered claret jug. The air inside the handle supplies an added touch of elegance. Designed by Frank Thrower and made by Dartington Glass, England

Port decanter on a foot, thinly blown; with matching glass. Designed by Ronald Stennett-Willson and made by Wedgwood Glass, England

The 'Victoria' service. Designed by Frank Thrower and made by Dartington Glass, England

A simple modern service with a heavy foot. Made at the Peill and Pützler Glassworks, Germany

Wine glasses made in clear crystal with an open foot. Designed by Ronald Stennett-Willson and made by Wedgwood Glass, England

A water set, with textured surface, hand blown in crystal. Designed by G. Baxter and made by Whitefriars Glass, England

A heavily textured square whisky decanter with lozenge stopper and matching tumblers, hand-made in lead crystal. Designed by G. Baxter and made by Dartington Glass, England

The traditional pottery Toby Jug made in glass. Designed by G. Baxter and made by Whitefriars Glass, England

A whisky decanter in clear crystal with a modern cutting. Part of the cutting is left unpolished so that the matt surface contrasts with the shiny. Designed by Ronald Stennett-Willson and made by Wedgwood Glass, England

Opposite top
Practical table and kitchen glass ware. Designed by Frank Thrower and made by Dartington Glass, England

Opposite bottom
A hand-made wine service in lead crystal with a simple flute cutting. Designed by Ronald Stennett-Willson and made by Wedgwood Glass, England

Robust, hand-made drinking glasses made by Boda Glassworks, Sweden

Plain decanter with air decorated stopper.
Designed by Ronald Stennett-Willson and
made by Wedgwood Glass, England

Oversize brandy balloons. Made in
Czechoslovakia

Pitcher or martini mixer with ice lip; with tumbler and pepper
and salt shaker. Designed by Severin Brørby and made by
Hadelands Glassworks, Norway

Finely blown elegant glasses in clear lead crystal with a
partially pressed stem on hand-made bowls. Designed by
Marc Lalique and made by Cristal Lalique, France

Beautifully made traditional glasses which, because they are well designed, are quite at home with modern glass. Made at the Moser Glassworks, Czechoslovakia

Wine glasses with clear bowl and foot with coloured air stem. Designed by Ronald Stennett-Willson and made by Wedgwood Glass, England

A table service in a simple shape with an interesting treatment to the bottom of the bowl. Designed by Severin Brørby and made by Hadelands Glassworks, Norway

A clear glass goblet with heavy bowl decorated with a single air bubble, with a tooled stem and foot. Designed by Ronald Stennett-Willson and made by Wedgwood Glass, England

A set of bar glasses with decanter and ice bucket in clear glass decorated with a single air bubble. Designed by Sidse Werner and made by Holmegaard, Denmark

A bowl, sundae glasses and plate with an all-over decoration coming from the mould. Designed by Oiva Toikka and made by Arabia, Finland

Opposite
A hand blown glass in three sizes with an unusual decorative stem. Designed by Oiva Toikka and made by Arabia, Finland

Decanter and glasses from a lead crystal wine service. Designed by G. Baxter and made by Whitefriars Glass, England

A range of very elegant completely hand-made glasses. Designed by Per Lütken and made by Holmegaard of Denmark

Ship's decanter with matching glasses in lead crystal, hand-cut and hand-polished. Designed by Ronald Stennett-Willson and made by Wedgwood Glass, England

Making a bowl

Most pieces of glass which are intended for use as bowls or vases are made by being blown into a mould and the edge finished in the way a wine glass is finished; that is, the edge is cracked off and then either melted, or if it is too thick, it is ground and polished. When glass makers talk of a piece being made 'freehand' (some say 'offhand' or 'driven') they mean that a mould, if used at all, gives only partial shape to the piece and the finished object is given its shape by the manipulations of the glass maker. The edge may have been cut with shears and polished in the glory hole, or, as in the case of the bowl shown here, may have the shape and the edge formed solely by the hand and the limited tools of the glass maker.

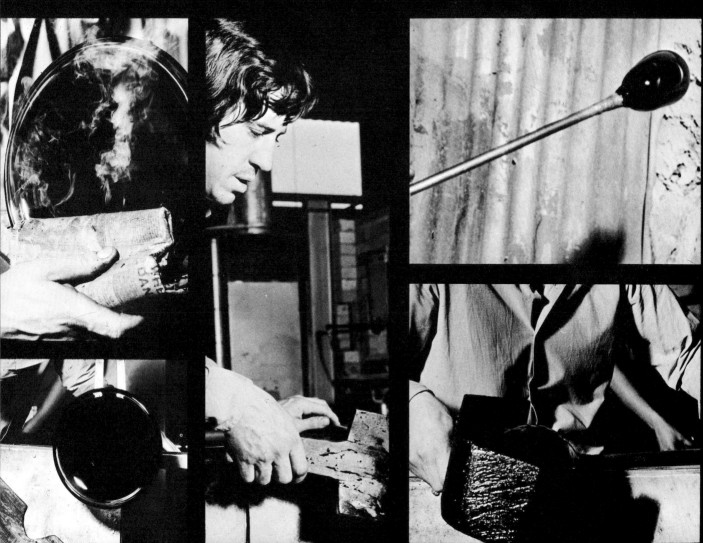

A ball of glass has been gathered and shaped. In this case it is coloured glass and the glassmaker goes to the furnace to gather over a layer of clear glass to add to it

The ball is 'blocked' into shape. The tool used is a cup of wood which is constantly dipped in water

The ball is then flattened by manipulation against a piece of wood. This is done in such a way that the colour stays in the centre leaving a rim of clear glass.

The flattened ball is expanded by spinning. The iron is rolled on the arms of the chair and centrifugal force produces an increase in size

The bowl continues to grow and the fingers and thumb of the glass maker, protected by wet newspaper, coax it into its final shape. At this point the glass maker has to use delicate control so that the piece does not distort and cease to be perfectly round. This process continues until the bowl is cool enough to hold the final shape

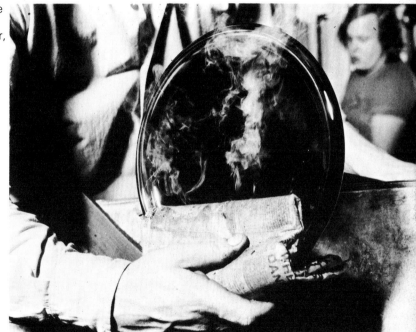

The bowl is now finished and the 'tool' is used to cut down the glass close to the iron. This is to ensure that when the finished piece is broken off the iron, there will be the minimum of glass to be ground away

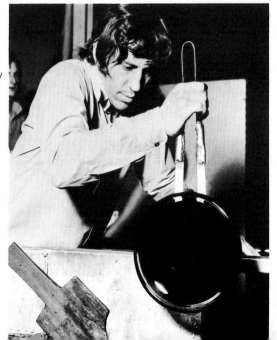

The simplest of cuts produces a formal leaf pattern on this lead crystal bowl and vase. Designed by Sigurd Persson and made by Kosta Glassworks, Sweden

There can hardly be a household which does not have at least one bowl or vase made of glass. In recent years there has been an effort by factories making modern glass to make pieces which are functional as bowls and vases but which can also be objects of decoration and in some cases, works of art.

To achieve this aim, glass from the more traditional factories usually used cutting. All means of decorating glass, apart from applying enamels by painting or transfer, attack the surface or skin. The glass cutter does this by using stone or carborundum wheels to grind away part of the glass. The part which is 'cut' like this is then polished, either by hand using a cork wheel with very fine abrasive or, more usually, by acid. Cutting thus exploits one of the properties of glass, its ability to reflect light, by creating extra polished surfaces.

Clear glass vases. Reversed, these can be used as candlesticks. Designed by Frank Thrower and made by Dartington Glass, England

Widely flared low bowl with solid circular base in clear crystal. Made by Steuben Glass, U.S.A.

Opposite top
Decanters, jug and ice bucket in clear glass with hand trailed bands of green and blue glass. Made by Schott-Zwiesel Glassworks, Germany

Opposite bottom
A group of glasses entitled 'The Complete Imbiber'. Designed by Frank Thrower and made by Dartington Glass, England

Hand-made lead crystal orchid vases. Designed by Atelier Leichlingen and made by Glashütte Leichlingen, Germany

These orchid and specimen vases have a very simple but effective gather of glass, coloured over clear. Made by Daum, France

On following colour pages
Square and rectangular vases in clear crystal in various sizes with a simple blue trailed glass decoration. Designed by Atelier Schott-Zwiesel and made by Schott-Zwiesel Glassworks, Germany

Bowl and dishes in full lead crystal, entitled 'Blue Fire'. The pattern is in blue and red. Designed by Göran Wärff and made by Kosta-Boda Glassworks, Sweden

Hand-made vases in blue and clear glass with a decoration formed by air bubbles. Designed by Atelier Schott-Zwiesel and made by Schott-Zwiesel Glassworks, Germany

High stemmed fruit and compote bowls in clear and coloured glass. The stems are hand-made and consist of solid and air filled parts. Designed by Ronald Stennett-Willson and made by Wedgwood Glass, England

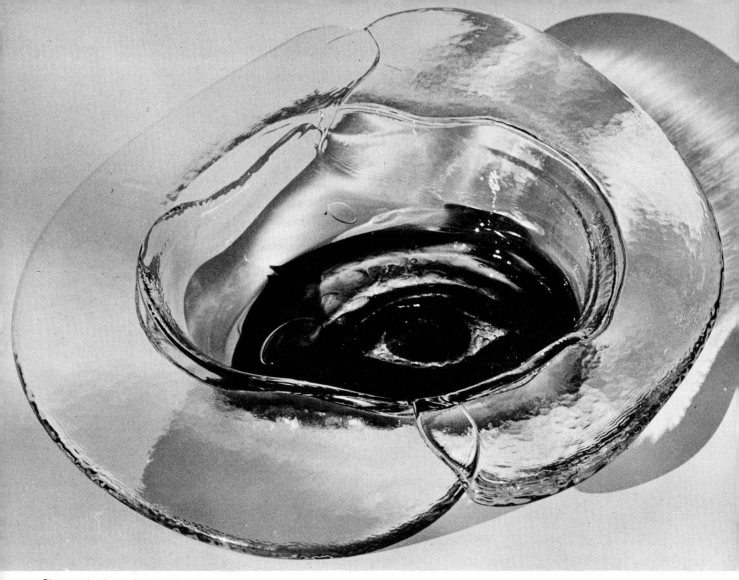

Clear and coloured crystal bowl making use of the 'brava' technique. Designed by Göran Wärff and made by Pukebergs Glassworks, Sweden

Hand-made ashtrays designed by Masakichi Awashima and made by Awashima Glass, Tokyo

On following colour pages
Hand-made plates with multi-coloured bands. Designed by Kay Franck and made by Wartsila, Nötsjö Glass, Finland

'Murrina': a mosaic vase. Designed by Ercole Barovier and made by Barovier and Toso, Italy

Hand-made champagne bucket and ice pail with blue glass trailed decoration. Designed by Atelier Schott-Zwiesel and made by Schott-Zwiesel Glassworks, Germany

Bowl and candlestick. Designed by Uno Westerberg and made by Pukebergs Glassworks, Sweden

Shallow bowls in clear glass. Designed by Uno Westerberg and made by Pukebergs Glassworks, Sweden

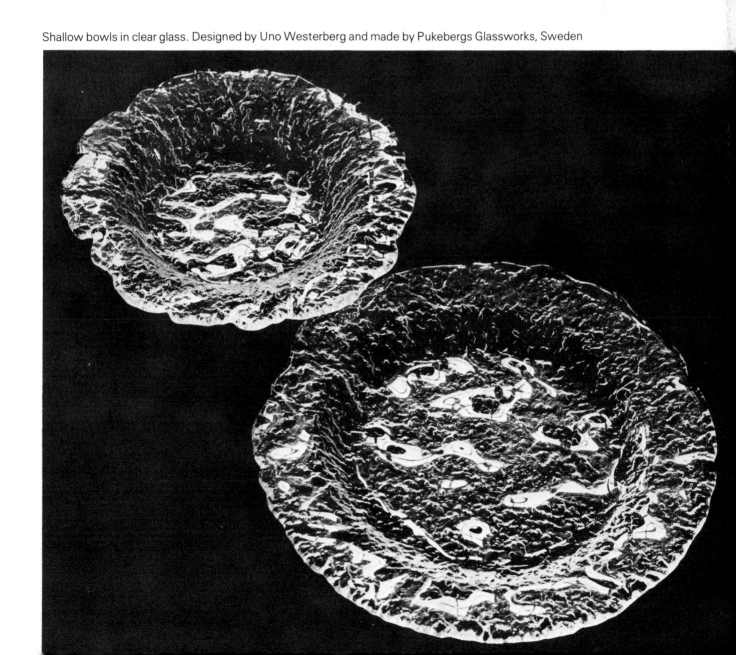

Opposite
Vase of heavy clear glass gathered over red. Designed by
Tamara Aladin and made by Riihimaen Lasi Oy, Finland

On following colour pages
Free-blown shape, clear with red stripes, by Marvin Lipovsky, California, U.S.A.

Group of small coloured bottles and vases by Edward Iglehart, Scotland

'Lava': a collection of bowls and vases in a soft colouring of opaque white and blue green. Designed by Per Lütken and made by Holmegaard of Denmark

Two vases in clear crystal. Designed by Olle Alberius and made by Orrefors of Sweden

Opposite top
Globular facetted vases. Designed by Asta Strömberg and
made by Strömbergshyttan, Sweden

Opposite bottom
These lead crystal bowls provide an example of restrained,
simple cutting on simple shapes. Designed by Joseph Pravec
and made by Bohemia Glassworks at Poděbrady,
Czechoslovakia

Roughing or making the first cuts on a wine glass bowl

Smoothing with a fine wheel and fine abrasive before final
hand-polishing

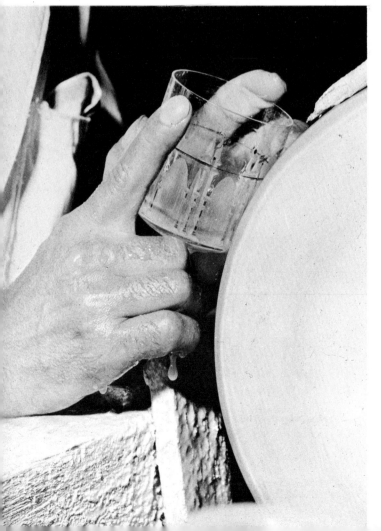

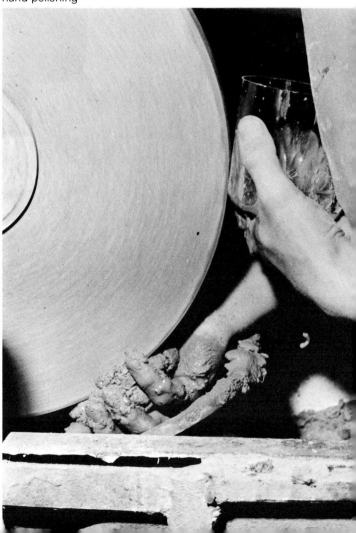

ee-blown bowls in
ansparent gold by
imrie Newcomb,
inois, U.S.A.

Heavy ashtray in clear crystal gathered over ruby. The cut flutes emphasize the contrast between the clear and coloured glass. Designed by Ronald Stennett-Willson and made by Wedgwood Glass, England

Composition in orange,
reen and amethyst
oloured glass by
Marvin Lipovsky,
California, U.S.A.

Lead crystal vase entitled 'Vase with a Thousand Eyes'. Designed by Asta Strömberg and made by Strömbergshyttan of Sweden

A rhythmic line cut on lead crystal bowl and vase. Designed by Olle Alberius and made by Orrefors of Sweden

Oppo
A group of vases and a bowl in a r
technique of inlaid 'lacework glass' ca
'Merletti'. Designed by Ove Thorsen
Birgitta Karlsson and made by Venini, I

Plate with background cutting of facets and cut
decoration of thistles. Designed by Josef Svarc
and made by Bohemia Glassworks, Poděbrady,
Czechoslovakia

A large vase in lead crystal, simply cut but with a
traditional feel about it. Made by Baccarat of
France

Vases with randomly applied colouring. Designed by G. Baxter and
made by hand by Whitefriars Glass, England

Large vases with textured surface, hand-made in colours cased by crystal. Designed by G. Baxter for Whitefriars Glass, England

'Membrane': a series of vases. Designed by Toni Zuccheri and made by Venini, Italy

Clear crystal bowl on pressed foot. The foot is in the form of three fishes and has a matt finish. Designed by Marie-Claude Lalique and made by Cristal Lalique, France

Simple vase with a hand-finished top in clear and coloured glass. Designed by Ronald Stennett-Willson and made by Wedgwood Glass, England

Heavy crystal vase with a fine textured surface. Designed by Marc Lalique and made by Cristal Lalique, France

Clear crystal vase with applied decoration. Designed by Don Pollard and made by Steuben, U.S.A.

Two vases, slightly opaque white with applied black decoration. Designed by Ercole Barovier and made by Barovier and Toso, Italy

'Neomurrine' vase. Designed by Ercole Barovier and made by Barovier and Toso, Italy

Candlesticks

e drawn stem
ndlesticks in four
es and made in clear
d coloured glass.
signed by Ronald
ennett-Willson and
de by Wedgwood
ass, England

It is unlikely that glass was used to any great extent for holding candles, magnificent glass chandeliers being an exception, until, paradoxically, candles were no longer a necessity and became decorative.

The gentle wavering light of candles, with glass picking up, reflecting and varying this light, is a happy combination, particularly at mealtimes.

Modern candlesticks using coloured glass and coloured candles become part of the table decoration and some designers make it possible to use flowers and candles in one piece of glass.

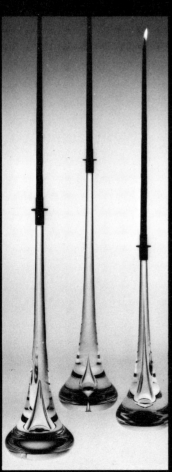

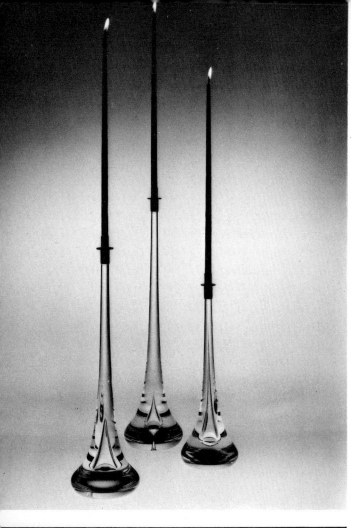

Hand-made candlesticks, the design of which echoes the way glass flows when semi-liquid. The internal air adds elegance. Made by Daum of France

A 'wind light' in a simple shape with a thick clear base over red glass. Designed by Tamara Aladin and made by Riihimaen Lasi Oy, Finland

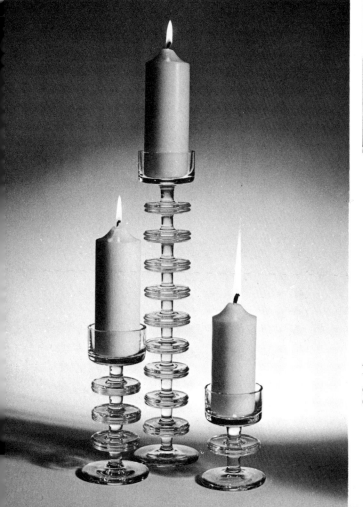

A candlestick made in a variety of sizes requiring patient and skilful work: the largest size (centre here) calls for twenty-one pieces of glass to be gathered. Designed by Ronald Stennett-Willson and made by Wedgwood Glass, England

The solid stem enclosing a tear-drop of air over the elegant domed foot makes this a satisfying piece. Made by Steuben Glass, U.S.A.

These candlesticks have what is known as a 'straw stem'; that is, they are hollow. Designed by Ronald Stennett-Willson and made by Wedgwood Glass, England

Candlesticks which become flower vases when reversed. Designed by Frank Thrower and made by Dartington Glass, England

A 'wind light' in two pieces with textured surface in clear glass. Designed by Ronald Stennett-Willson and made by Wedgwood Glass, England

To make an object such as a bird, working free-hand, requires very great skill, and to interpret the wish of the designer requires more skill, but the test of a really good glass maker is to make something like a bird to a predetermined pattern and to make this object over and over again with the differences between pieces remaining almost infinitesimal. This is the essence of craftmanship. The task requires sustained attention and results not in a series of mechanically exact objects, but in creations which look alike but at the same time are individual and distinctive, because of the concentration and care which come through the craftsman's hands.

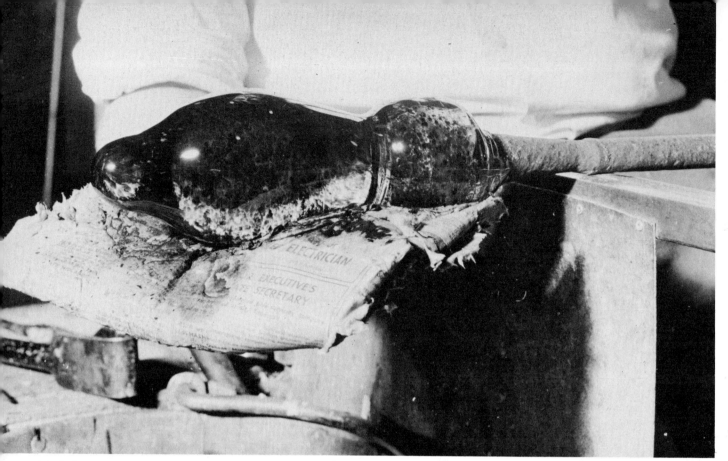

A ball of clear glass has been gathered from the furnace and rolled in grains of brown glass. This is then taken to the glory hole and the grains are melted into the surface of the ball. When this surface has been worked absolutely smooth, a layer of clear glass is gathered over and it is now given the basic shape by the glass maker's hand. Care has to be taken to ensure that the grains are melted fully into the surface because any slight roughness could trap air and cause bubbles when the second gather is made

The tool is used to cut down the glass on the iron

The glass is allowed to fall so far and is then caught with shears and the tail pulled out. At this instant the glass maker has to grab at the glass with his shears and if he misses this moment, the glass, which is still plastic, will fall too far and be distorted

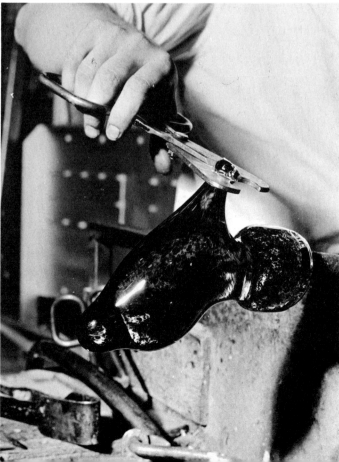

As it is worked on, the glass will cool down and the glory hole will have to be used to re-heat and soften it. The glass maker has to carry out his important manipulations within the few minutes between the time that the glass is too liquid and the moment when it has cooled to the point when it is no longer soft enough to be worked. While making a piece like this he will occasionally cool it a little with a jet of cool, compressed air, and, when necessary, re-heat it in the glory hole

The beak is pulled out

Finally, the eyes are added and at the same time, while the glass is still soft enough, the bird is pulled into its final shape. The result is a partridge in clear glass with brown speckles

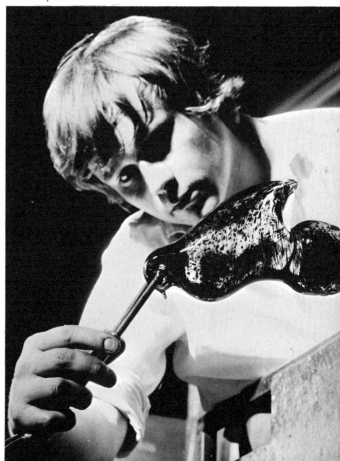

Figures

'The Great Whale': a hand-made piece in clear crystal. Designed by Paul Schulze and made by Steuben Glass, U.S.A.

Most glass makers at some time, particularly when learning, attempt to make a figure of some kind. The results of these efforts have a name: they are known as glass makers' 'friggers'. Some of these made long ago can be found nowadays in antique shops. They were frequently made to sell to visitors to the glassworks or for amusement. It is very rare that any figures made in this way have any real quality, for they are usually merely examples of one aspect of a particular glass maker's skill.

Glass as a medium does not allow much detail in design unless it is pressed, that is, mechanically moulded, so the most attractive figures are those which try to express the essence of the bird or animal modelled rather than attempt a caricature or a strict representation.

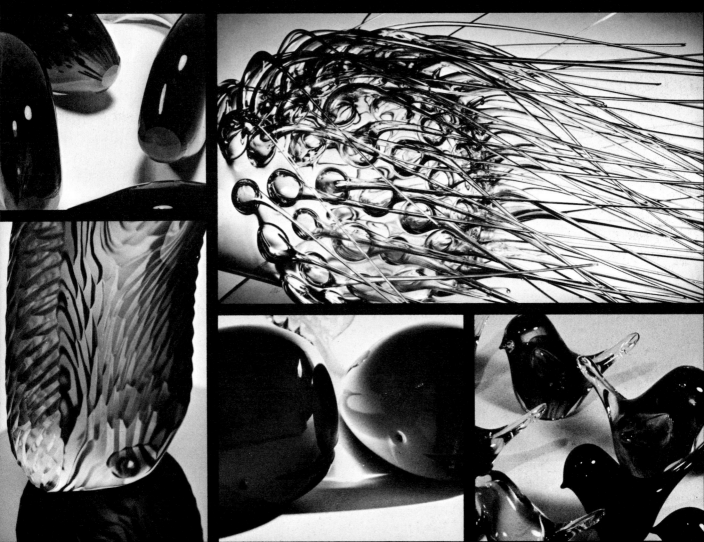

Partridge and duck, both made free-hand in clear glass with brown speckles. Designed by Ronald Stennett-Willson and made by Wedgwood Glass, England

An owl in coloured glass. The basic colour is light fawn with dark brown speckles applied. Designed by Ronald Stennett-Willson and made by Wedgwood Glass, England

An aloof-looking cat in clear crystal. Made by Baccarat, France

Opposite
An owl and a cat in clear crystal.
Made by Steuben Glass, U.S.A.

Whales created free-hand in clear or coloured glass. Designed by Ronald Stennett-Willson and made by Wedgwood Glass, England

A hedgehog made from technical glass in Czechoslovakia by Vera Liskova, using an oxygen flame

Fish made free-hand in coloured glass with pale oatmeal colour under greenish black. Designed by Ronald Stennett-Willson and made by Wedgwood Glass, England

A bull and cow sculpted from glass by Professor Klingg, Czechoslovakia

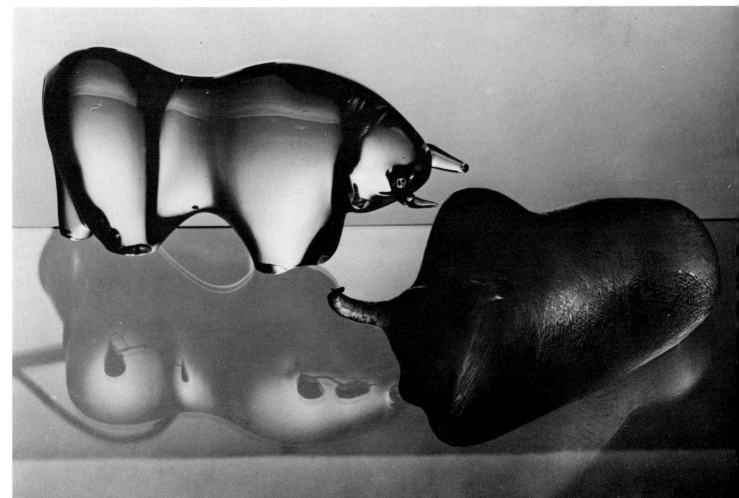

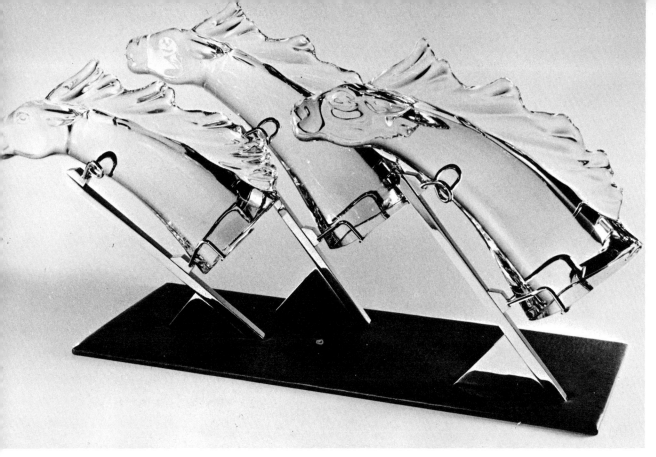

Large composition of horses with flowing manes. Made by Daum, France, in a limited edition

Large composition of wild duck in flight, in clear crystal. Made by Daum, France, in a limited edition

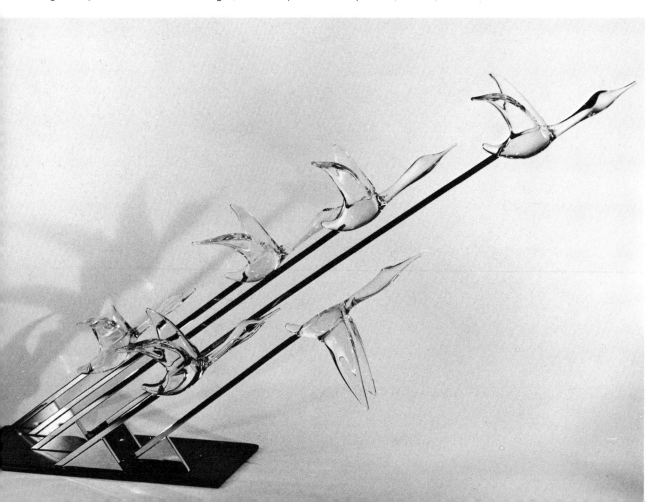

Penguin in clear crystal. Made by Baccarat,
France

Owl in clear crystal on glass base. Made by
Baccarat, France

Penguins made by hand in clear and coloured glass. Designed by Ronald Stennett-Willson and made by Wedgwood
Glass, England

Hedgehogs sculpted by cutting. Made in Czechoslovakia

A collection of sparrows made by hand in clear and coloured glass. Designed by Ronald Stennett-Willson and made by Wedgwood Glass, England

A pugnacious looking boar in clear crystal. Made by Baccarat, France

A toad pressed in the Lalique technique. Designed by Marc Lalique and made by Cristal Lalique, France

Pigeon in the 'Primavera' finish, opaque white with black decoration. Designed by Ercole Barovier and made by Barovier and Toso, Italy

Snails in coloured glass. Designed by Ronald Stennett-Willson and made by Wedgwood Glass, England

...out and fly, a ...bination of crystal ...old. The internal air ...les have been ...e to a ...etermined pattern. ...ly is 18 carat gold. ...gned by James ...ton and made by ...oen, U.S.A.

The equipment required to melt glass of a consistently good quality is very expensive and until recently was available in a form which would allow only a small amount of glass to be melted. It was thus very difficult for an individual to set up a workshop or studio in which he could prepare his own material. However, during the last fifteen years progress has been made and it is now possible to do the melting in equipment suitable for one or two people working together. Also, a

number of colleges in America and this country have started departments in which students can learn to design and make glass with the aid of a small furnace.

There would seem to be considerable advantage to be gained by two or three designer-craftsmen getting together and forming small glass workshops. This would make it more feasible for individual pieces of glass to be made which could be a little more sophisticated and well finished.

Leaf goblets made in black, clear and opaque glass by Jane Gilchrist, England

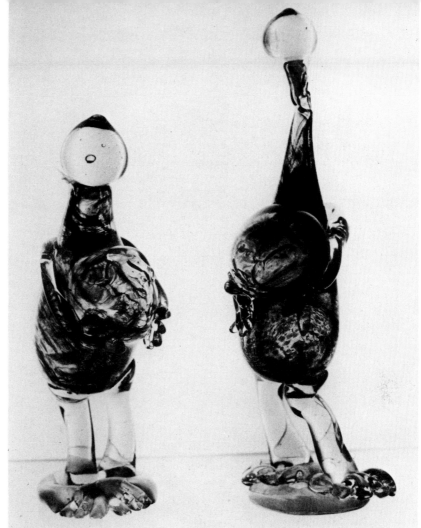

Green and brown figurine
bottles by Annette Meech,
England

Free-blown bowl in orange
with blue and green patterning
by Jane Gilchrist, England

93

Free-blown vase, opaque white with amber decoration. Made by John Cook, Leicester Polytechnic, England

Above
'Emergence XV': a glass sculpture by Dominick Labino, U.S.A.

Composition in clear glass by W. Bernstein, Burnsville, North Carolina, U.S.A.

'Projector 1': a composition in
blown glass and steel by
Edward Iglehart, Scotland

Goblets with variegated
coloured bowls on clear stem
and feet by Annette Meech,
England

Free-hand opaque white vase with black trailed pattern. Made by W. Bernstein, Burnsville, North Carolina, U.S.A.

Below
'Anatomie Surréaliste': a glass sculpture by Dominick Labino, U.S.A.

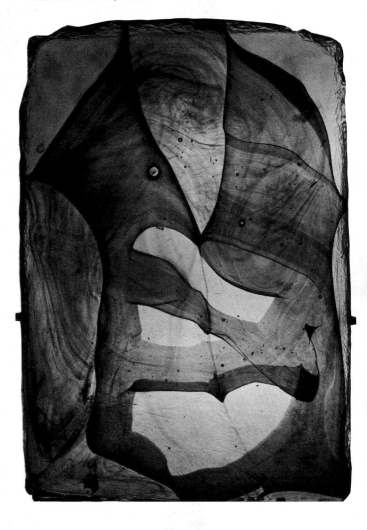

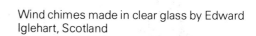
Wind chimes made in clear glass by Edward Iglehart, Scotland

Opposite
Multi-coloured pieces designed and made by Michael Harris at his small but commercial glass factory, Isle of Wight Studio Glass Ltd

Free-hand clear bowl with pattern in amethyst, brown and blue. Made by Jane Gilchrist, England

Two goblets with clear bowls and coloured stems made free-hand by Annette Meech, England

On following colour page
'Pluto': a paperweight in a limited edition with both colour and air used internally. Designed by Colin Terris and made by Peter Holmes at Caithness Glass, Scotland

'Orange Coral': a paperweight which uses the same technique. Designed by Colin Terris and made by Caithness Glass, Scotland

Solid paperweight with an internal spiral of colour and air obtained by the use of copper. Designed by Atelie Schott-Zwiesel and made by Schott-Zwiesel, Germany

Paperweights

Glass is a popular medium for paperweights, and has been for a long time. There are many collectors who have specialized collections from particular periods or of certain types. Millefiori paperweights using coloured glass cane in complicated internal patterns, or with glass flowers enclosed in clear glass, have been made in many countries. A fascinating technique is the enclosure of a white sulphide cast in clear crystal, which allows for the representation of a head or emblem to be made in very precise detail.

Modern paperweights tend to use air or colour. Glass as a solid light-ensnaring lump is fascinating but is even more fascinating to trap air or colour inside. This, I am sure, is the sole *raison d'être* of many paperweights.

100

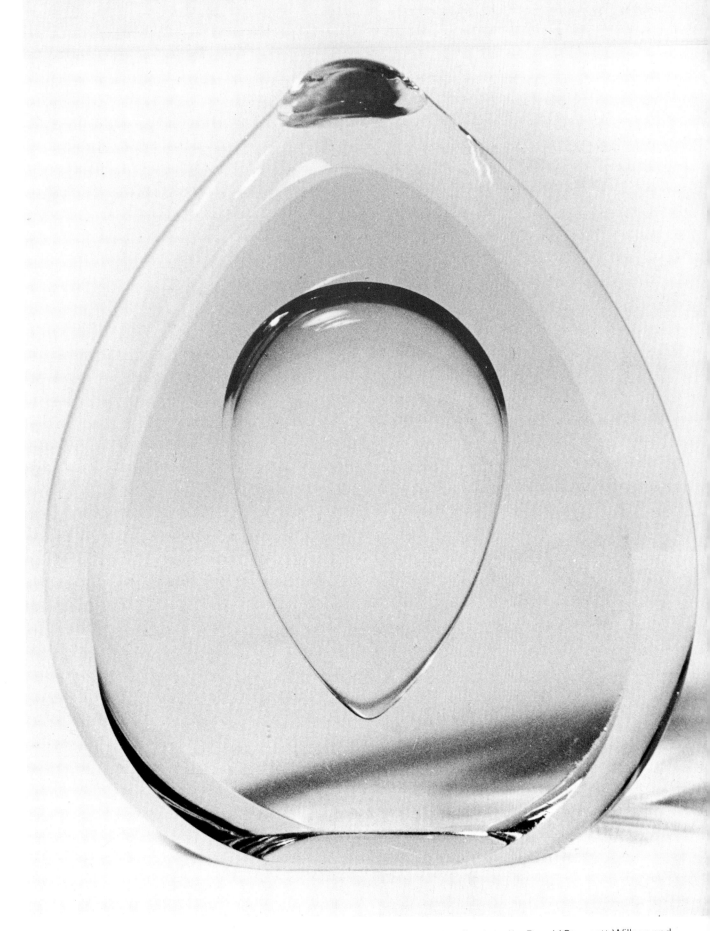

'Valentine': a flat clear crystal paperweight with controlled air bubble. Designed by Ronald Stennett-Willson and made by Wedgwood Glass, England

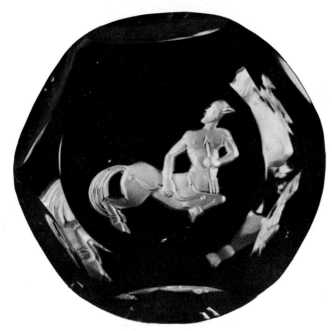

One of a series of paperweights incorporating a sulphide cast of a zodiacal sign. The piece was made by Baccarat, who perfected the technique

A drawing of a lead crystal paperweight which has a colour gathered over clear glass. The colour is cut away in parts to make a lens effect through which the engraving is magnified. Made by Webb Corbett, England

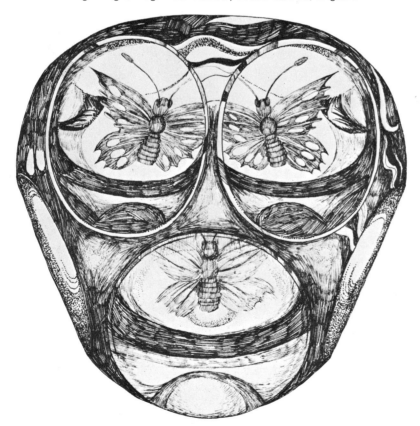

On following colour pages
'Polar': a bowl in clear and colours with a sculptural quality. Designed by Göran Wärff and made by Kosta Glassworks, Sweden

Crystal 'scrapers'. Designed by Lars Hellston and made by Orrefors Glassworks, Sweden

An opaque yellow vase with opaque blue decoration covered in clear crystal. Designed by Göran Wärff and made by Kosta Glassworks, Sweden

Clear crystal paperweights with air bubbles. Made by Kosta-Boda Glassworks, Sweden

Clear crystal paperweights with air bubbles. Designed by Atelier Schott-Zwiesel and made by Schott-Zwiesel, Germany

A solid piece of crystal, cut and polished to catch the light. Made by Baccarat of France

'Moon': a paperweight made in a limited edition using both colour and air internally. Designed by Colin Terris and made by Peter Holmes at Caithness Glass, Scotland

Clear crystal paperweight with controlled air pattern, made large enough to serve as a door stopper. Designed by Ronald Stennett-Willson and made by Wedgwood Glass, England

On following colour pages
A combined candlestick and flower vase in clear glass. Designed by Frank Thrower and made by Dartington Glass, England

'Woman's Dance': a vase in blue and red, with the pattern etched on over and underlay. Designed by Ann Wärff and made by Kosta Glassworks, Sweden

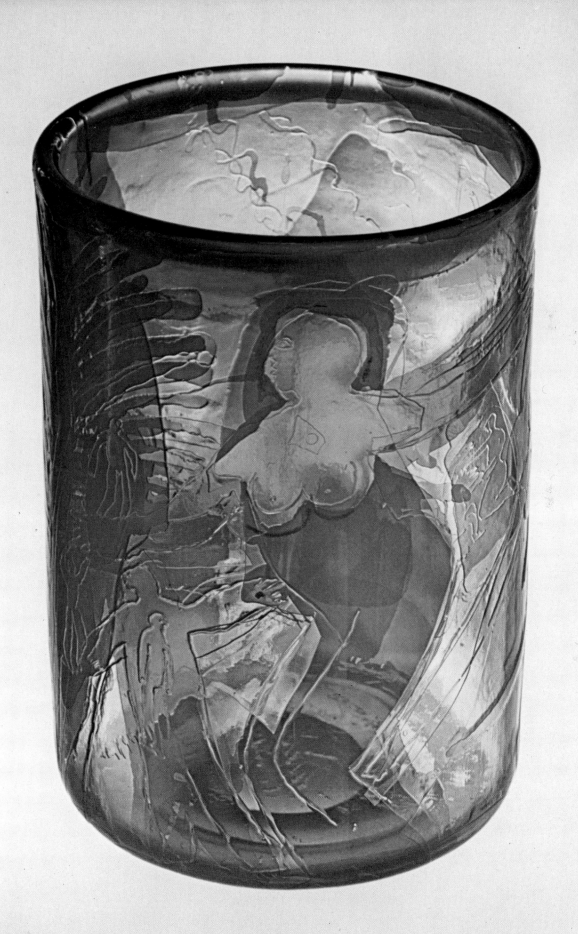

Unique pieces

wl and vase in clear
stal. Designed by
e Alberius and made
he Orrefors
ssworks, Sweden

In some glass factories provision is made for the designer to work as an individual. Production facilities and the time of one or two highly skilled craftsmen are made available. Where such enlightened management has done this it has been of considerable advantage to the factory.

Work of this nature, bringing together the experience of the designer and the skill of the glass maker, with mutual respect for each other's contribution, increases the possibilities for both to extend their ability, knowledge and technique. This in turn has an effect on the general quality of glass making in the factory, because new ways of working discovered in response to the demands of an adventurous design can be applied to general production. Also, the sight of a highly skilled craftsman at work stimulates a desire to emulate him.

On the following pages we see examples of the work of individual designers working in established commercial factories. The suitability of glass as a rich and satisfying medium for sculpture is also illustrated. Many of these pieces find their way into private collections and become increasingly valuable.

Opaque white vase with random colourings
and clear crystal overlay. Designed by Per
Lütken and made by Holmegaard Glassworks,
Denmark

Clear crystal bowl. Designed by Per Lütken
and made by Holmegaard Glassworks,
Denmark

Opposite
Bottle and bowl by Mikko Merikallio, Finland

'Apollo': a group in three sizes in a limited edition, in clear crystal with internal air decoration. Designed by Ronald Stennett-Willson and made by Wedgwood Glass, England

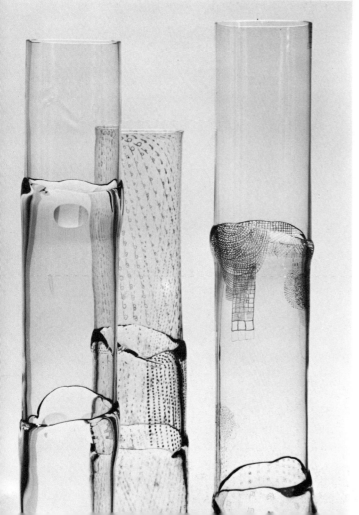

Sculptures decorated with diamond point engraving and gold. Designed by Oiva Toikka and made by Nötsjö Glass, Finland

Opposite
A sophisticated sculpture by Jan Johansson in a limited edition of 200 pieces. Made in clear crystal by Orrefors Glassworks, Sweden

Orrefors Sweden Art in Crystal
Metropolis 1/73
Limited Edition No 1 of 200

Sculpture in a mixture of clear and coloured
crystal. Designed by Göran Wärff and
made by Kosta Glassworks, Sweden

'Saying of Confucius': an elegant sculpture
from Steuben Glass, U.S.A. The glass
design is by Donald Pollard and the
engraving design by Cho Chung-yung

Opposite
A vase in which large cut olives highlight orange
and black stripes on clear crystal. Designed by
Olle Alberius and made by Orrefors Glassworks,
Sweden

'Meditation': a figure in reddish-brown amber coloured glass. Designed by Jean-Pierre Demardi and made by Daum of France

A pair of simple pieces which together form one sculpture. Designed by Robert Rigot and made by Baccarat of France

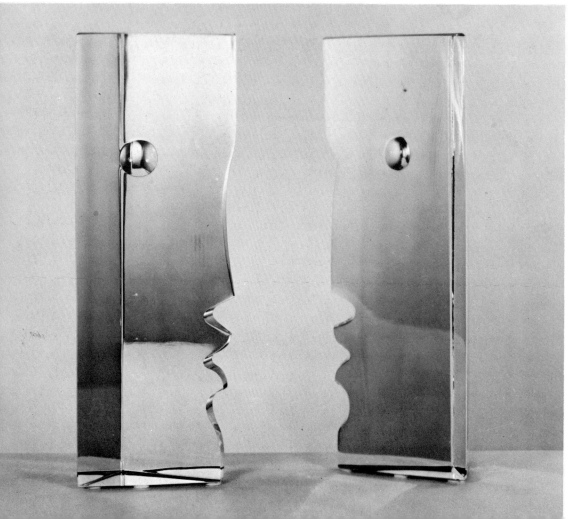

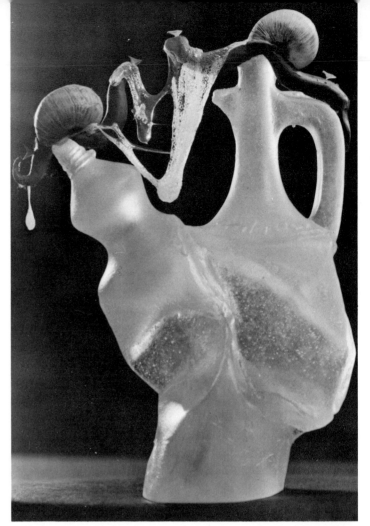

'L'Important c'est la Rose': a work
designed by Salvador Dali in uranium
orange and produced in a limited edition of
150 by Daum of France

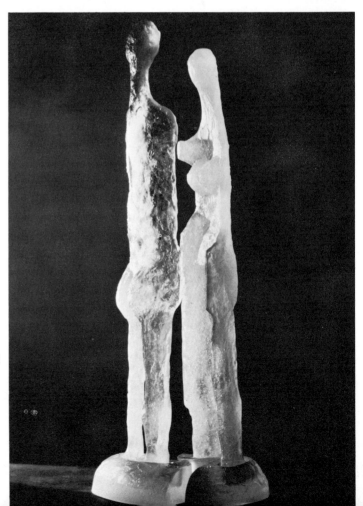

A pair of figures in clear glass entitled 'Un et
Une'. Designed by Robert Couterier and
made by Daum of France in a limited
edition of 100 pieces

A head sculpted by cutting and polishing a piece of clear crystal. Designed by Sven Palmqvist and made by Orrefors Glassworks, Sweden

A simple sculpture in clear crystal. Designed by Sven Palmqvist and made by Orrefors Glassworks, Sweden

Opposite
Sculpture with a greenish blue stem and a ball head in blue, black, orange and spongy pale blue. Designed by Oiva Toikka and made by Nötsjö Glass, Finland

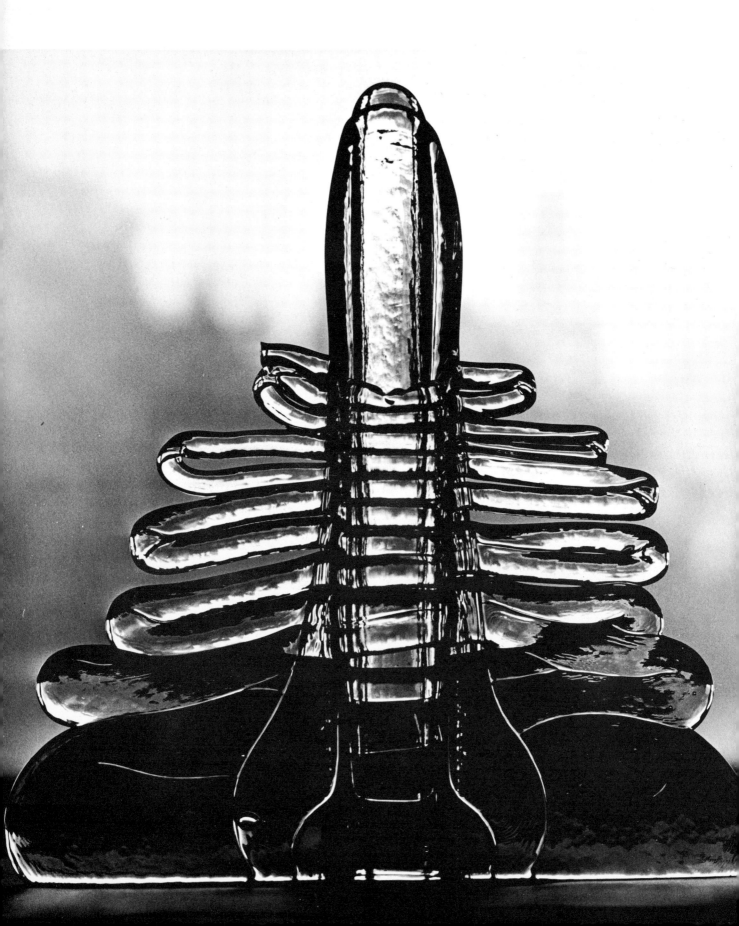

A sculpture showing the plastic quality of glass. Designed by Bertil Vallén and made by Kosta Glassworks, Sweden

A clear crystal sculpture entitled
'Counterpoise'. Designed by Donald
Pollard and made by Steuben Glass, U.S.A.

'Romeo and Juliet': a sculpture in clear crystal, polished, engraved and cut. Designed
by Vicke Lindstrand and made by Kosta Glassworks, Sweden

Engraving and sandblasting

As with cutting, the engraver obtains his result by taking away part of the surface of the glass. Engravers tend to fall quite firmly into two groups: those who use a wheel, usually of copper moistened with fine oil carrying a fine abrasive; and those who 'stipple' using a diamond or tungsten point. Diamond point engraving depends for its effect on a light-and-shade appearance, whereas copper wheel engraving shows a more three dimensional result. A difference between the techniques is that with copper wheel engraving the glass is taken to the small lathe, but with diamond point, the tool is taken to the glass. Many of the wheel engravers are now using diamond-impregnated wheels in portable tools like a dentist's drill and for large scale work, a stone wheel. There are signs that the number of engravers in Britain is increasing, and one hopes that it is the same in other countries because it is a medium which has tremendous scope for the designer-craftsman.

Sandblasting involves taking away the surface of the glass with an abrasive projected in a jet of compressed air. It is generally used as a coarse form of cutting or engraving, yet it can give extremely fine detail.

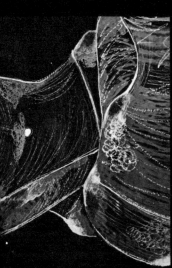

A goblet being engraved by the copper wheel technique. The smooth copper wheel is moistened with fine oil bearing a very fine abrasive. In this process the glass is taken to the wheel, whereas in the diamond point method the tool is taken to the glass

Oppos
Another bowl engraved by Peter Dreiser, England. La
areas of the glass have been cut away to leave pattern in re

A plate on which both sandblasting and engraving have been used to achieve the decoration. Made by Elly Eliades, England

A bowl engraved by Peter Dreiser, England

Opposite
'Earth Fruits': a globe with figures in blue and sandblasted underlay
Designed by Ann Wärff and made by Kosta Glassworks, Sweden

'The Orator': a vase engraved by Colin Terris, Caithness Glass, Scotland

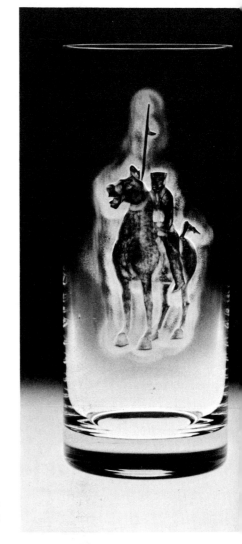

A vase engraved with a Kandtu Horse
(from the Chinese Exhibition) by Colin
Terris, Caithness Glass, Scotland

129

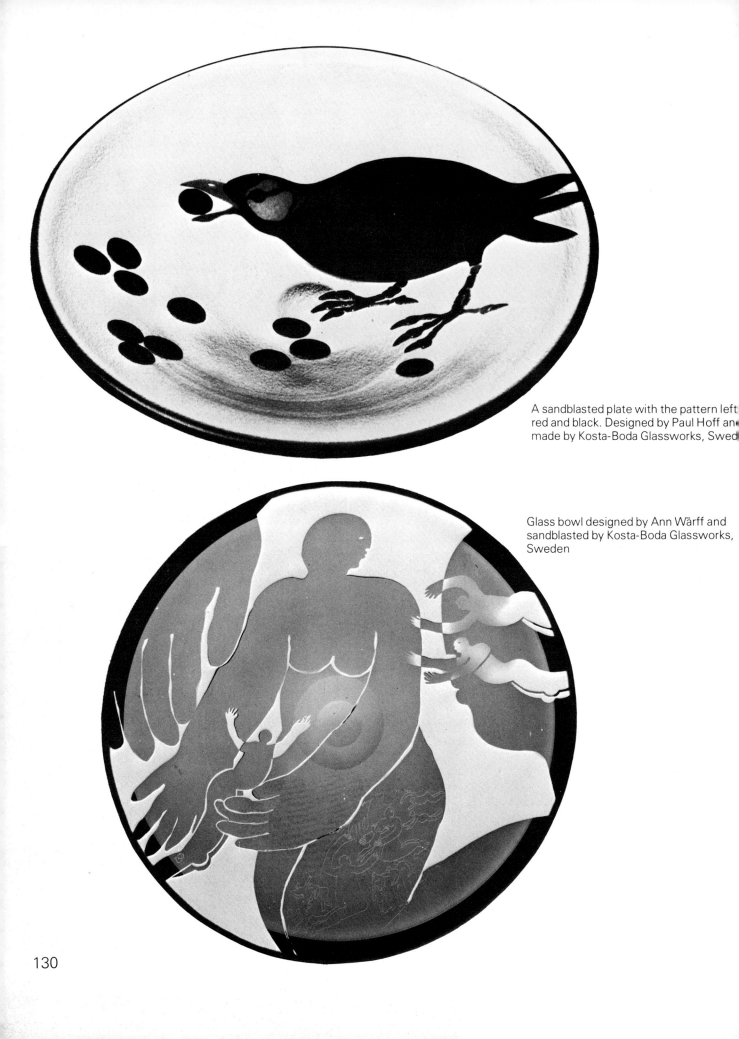

A sandblasted plate with the pattern left red and black. Designed by Paul Hoff and made by Kosta-Boda Glassworks, Sweden

Glass bowl designed by Ann Wärff and sandblasted by Kosta-Boda Glassworks, Sweden

Square bowl, sandblasted. Designed
by Bertil Vallén and made by
Kosta-Boda Glassworks, Sweden

A combination of copper wheel and
diamond point engraving is used to
decorate this piece of crystal made
by Steuben Glass, U.S.A. The glass
design is by Paul Schulze and the
engraving design by Donald Crowley

On following colour pages
Dish with orange centre and brown
trailed decoration. Designed by Olle
Alberius and made by Orrefors
Glassworks, Sweden

Crystal sculptures. Designed by Olle
Alberius and made by Orrefors
Glassworks, Sweden

Bowl, vase and paperweights.
Designed and made by Michael
Harris, Isle of Wight Studio Glass Ltd

131

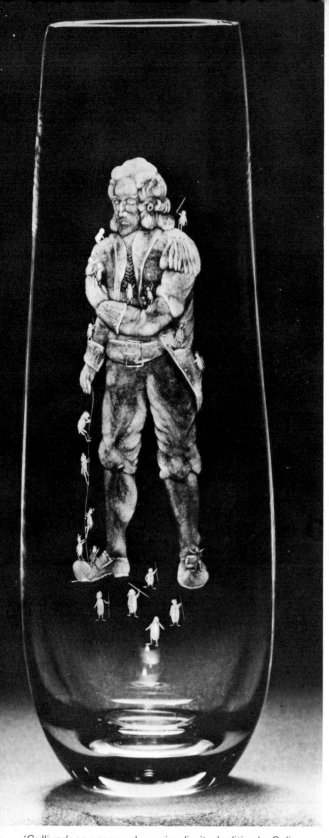

'Gulliver': an engraved vase in a limited edition by Colin Terris, Caithness Glass, Scotland

Two Females': a vase engraved by Bruce Walker, Scotland

An engraving of weasels on a low bowl by Bruce Walker, Scotland

'Birthday Present': an engraved goblet by Peter Dreiser, England

On following colour pages
'Quintessence': a luxurious piece in crystal and gold made in a limited edition of five by Steuben Glass, U.S.A. The glass design is by Paul Schulze and the gold design by Patricia Davidson

A vase in blue and clear crystal with controlled air and colour patterns within the walls of the glass. Designed by Ronald Stennett-Willson and made under his supervision at Wedgwood Glass, England

Vase with a sea-creature motif within the walls. The colour is a varying blue-green. Designed by Ronald Stennett-Willson and made under his supervision at Wedgwood Glass, England

135

Full lead crystal vase designed by
Lisa Bauer and Sigurd Persson
and made by Kosta-Boda
Glassworks, Sweden

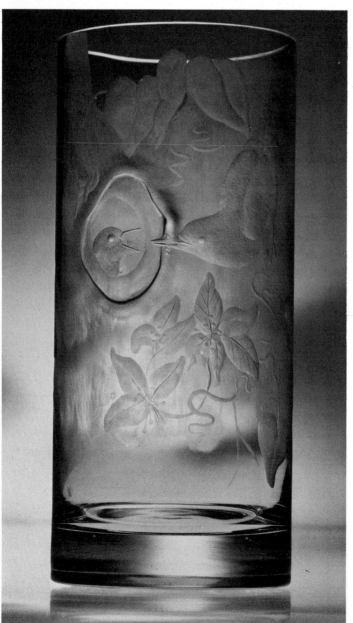

A vase with a copper wheel engraving of a nuthatch
feeding its young by Colin Terris, Caithness Glass,
Scotland

On following colour pages
A lighting fitting composed of modular glass forms.
Designed and made by Barovier and Toso, Italy

Window in the Almshouse at Linköping, made from
coloured pieces of hand-made glass. Designed by
Erik Höglund and made by Kosta Glassworks,
Sweden

Large chandelier of multi-coloured square glass
parts. Designed by Barovier and Toso, Italy

138

'The Drunkards': an engraved tankard by Bruce Walker, Scotland

A crystal prism made by Steuben Glass, U.S.A. The glass design is by George Thompson and the engraving design by Alexander Seidel

'Otter in the Burn': a decanter engraved with a diamond burr by Bruce Walker, Scotland

Deeply engraved vase in green glass with the decoration left in relief. By Peter Dreiser, England

Diamond point engraving by John Coughlan, England

A commemorative decanter engraved by diamond point by John Coughlan, England

An engraved glass panel by John Hutton, England

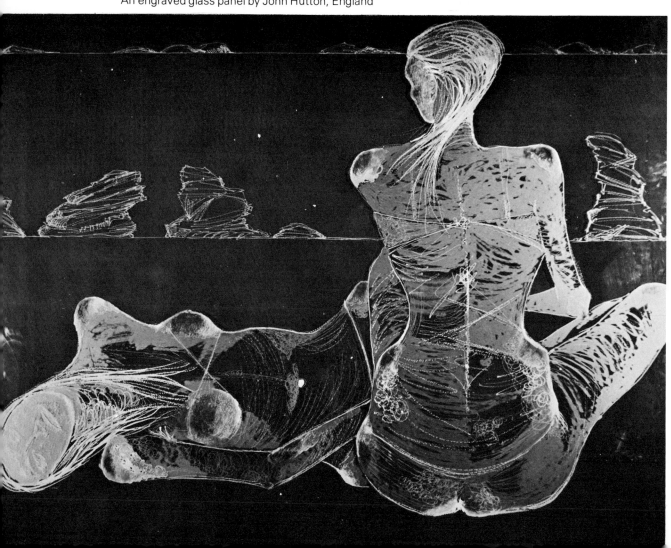

An engraved tankard by Josephine Majella,
England

'Sitting Nude': a large goblet by John
Hutton, England

143

'Safari': a full lead crystal vase designed by Vicke Lindstrand and made by Kosta Glassworks, Sweden

Opposite
Opaque white bowl with yellow decoration covered in clear crystal. Designed by Göran Wärff and made by Kosta Glassworks, Sweden

145

An engraved plate by Josephine
Majella, England

A copper wheel engraved vase in the
traditional style, made in
Czechoslovakia

146

Pair of decanters presented to H.R.H. Princess Margaret. Designed by Ronald Stennett-Willson and made by Wedgwood Glass, England

A fan shaped vase with an engraving of a glass blower. Designed by David Smith and made by Webb Corbett, England

'A Midsummer Night's Dream': designed by Vicke Lindstrand and made by Kosta Glassworks, Sweden

Opposite
'Wessex Nightfall': a b
designed and engraved
Laurence Whistler, Engl

Opposite bott
'A Dazzling Darkness': anot
bowl designed and engra
by Laurence Whistler, Engl

Copper wheel engraving of
fisherman on a vase made
Strömbergshyttan, Swede
The glass design is by Asta
Strömberg and the engravi
design by Rune Strand

'Fly in the Dark': a piece suggested by Agamemnon's Tomb at Mycenae, designed and engraved by Laurence Whistler, England

The most obvious use of glass architecturally is in the numerous stained glass windows in churches in this country and on the Continent. During the last few years it has been possible to see glass used imaginatively by architects in modern glass windows. Sometimes the glass is set in the traditional lead, sometimes in cement and occasionally in epoxy resin.

This seems to happen more commonly on the Continent. In Germany, for example, architects building industrial offices or factories are encouraged to spend a certain percentage of the cost on the artistic appearance.

There can be no doubt that this is an area where the use of modern glass has by no means been fully exploited. There are tremendous opportunities in this direction.

Here are just a few illustrations of glass used to decorate windows and walls and to make modern chandeliers.

DA GLORIAM DEO

Opposite
A window in the hall of the Worshipful Company of Dyers, commemorating the 500th anniversary of the granting to the company of its first charter of incorporation, 16 February 1471. Designed and partially engraved by Laurence Whistler and executed by T and W Ide Ltd, England

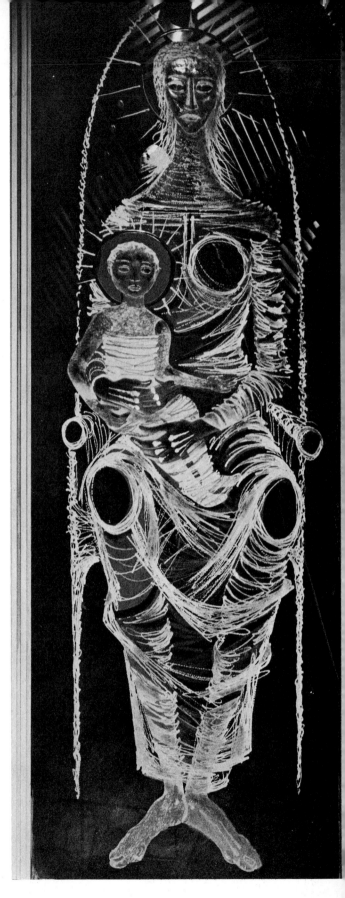

'Ophelia': detail from an engraved glass window in the Shakespeare Centre, Stratford on Avon. Designed and engraved by John Hutton

Madonna and child from the Great West Screen, Coventry Cathedral. Engraved by John Hutton

Lead crystal chandeliers. Designed by Jonas Hidle and made by Hadelands Glassworks, Norway

An illuminated sculpture in clear glass. Designed by Barbara Foscari and Sandro de Luigi and made by Barovier and Toso, Italy

Modern church lighting: floor chandelier and wall brackets in clear glass and iron. Designed by Erik Höglund and made by Boda Glassworks, Sweden

modern crystal chandelier composed of 900 parts in clear lead crystal. Designed by Jonas Hidle and made by
ovik Verk in co-operation with Hadelands Glassworks, Norway

Index

159